THE WISDOM OF THE ANCIENT EGYPTIANS

THE AUTHOR

William MacQuitty is a Fellow of the Royal Geographical Society, a Fellow of the Royal Photographical Society of Great Britain, an Honorary M.A. of the Queen's University, Belfast and was a film producer whose award winning films include A Night to Remember, *about the sinking of the* Titanic. *His books*—Abu Simbel, Irish Gardens, Buddha, Great Botanical Gardens of the World, Princess of Jade, The World in Focus, Island of Isis, Persia, the Immortal Kingdom, Our World in Colour *and most recently,* Ramesses the Great, Master of the World—*have won him international acclaim. He is also a major contributor to the new* Random House Encyclopaedia. *His book* Tutankhamun, The Last Journey, *is a current best seller and* The Wisdom of the Ancient Egyptians *is a complementary volume describing treasures of thought which more than match the material splendour that surrounded the boy king,* Tutankhamun.

Published by
New Directions

THE WISDOM OF THE
ANCIENT EGYPTIANS

SELECTED BY
WILLIAM MACQUITTY

A NEW DIRECTIONS BOOK

Manufactured in the United States of America
First published clothbound and as New Directions Paperbook 467
in 1978 by arrangement with Sheldon Press, London

Library of Congress Cataloging in Publication Data

Main entry under title:
The Wisdom of the ancient Egyptians.
   (A New Directions Book)
   (Wisdom series)
   1. Didactic literature, Egyptian—Translations
into English.   2. Didactic literature, English—
Translations from Egyptian.   I. MacQuitty, William.
II. Series: Wisdom series (New York).
PJ1959.W5   299'.31   78-6907
ISBN 0-8112-0701-3
ISBN 0-8112-0702-1 pbk.

New Directions Books are published for James Laughlin
by New Directions Publishing Corporation,
333 Sixth Avenue, New York 10014

TABLE OF CONTENTS

FOREWORD

THE ancient Egyptians were an artistic and imaginative people, but not of a notably philosophical turn of mind. They were practical and pragmatic, splendid at solving the immediate problems and difficulties which they encountered in life, but given less to theorizing or drawing general conclusions. In their mathematics, for example, they were not concerned at solving theoretical problems which had very little to do with the day-to-day activities of calculation in practical building works and in keeping accounts. Similarly, in the regulation of their daily lives they were not, as far as we can judge from surviving documents, concerned with abstract ideas of metaphysics and ethics. They were, however, great practitioners of what might now be termed 'horse-sense'. A long and settled civilization, nurtured in a peaceful society, gave plenty of opportunity for the formulation of a code of every-day morality which is expressed not only in the semi-autobiographical texts put up in the tombs of officials and nobles, but also in writings composed of didactic passages, aphorisms, guides for action, and general reflections on life.

The selection of sayings culled by William Mac-Quitty from what is usually called Egyptian 'wisdom' literature, demonstrates most clearly the sensible, practical, and yet essentially humane, attitude of the ancient Egyptian to life and to his fellow man. As revealed in these extracts from standard translations, the Egyptian was a person with whom we can easily feel a genuine sympathy. Mr MacQuitty clearly has this sympathy—born undoubtedly from his own deep understanding of other eastern cultures; for him the Egyptians are astute, sensible and full of humanity. The evidence speaks for itself; there need be no special pleading.

T. G. H. JAMES
Keeper of Egyptian Antiquities
British Museum

ACKNOWLEDGEMENTS

I WISH to thank Mr T. G. H. James, Keeper of Egyptian Antiquities, British Museum, who most kindly wrote the Foreword and checked my manuscript. His encouragement of interest in Egyptology has led many people to study this fascinating subject.

On the fiftieth anniversary of my first visit to Egypt I give special thanks to my Egyptian friends, to H.E. Adel Taher, Under Secretary of State in the Ministry of Tourism and to his Directors: Mr Aly Khala in Aswan, Mr Galal Ead in Luxor, Mr Mohamed Ibrahim in Cairo, Madame Nadia Ibrahim in Alexandria and Mr Sami el Masri in London, who together with their courteous colleagues have been so helpful. My deepest gratitude to H.E. Dr Gamal ed-Din Mukhtar, formerly Under Secretary of State in charge of the Antiquities Service, and to H.E. Mr Samih Anwar, the Egyptian Ambassador in London, also to the Egypt Exploration Society and its Secretary, Mary Crawford, for her help during my search through the Society's Library, and to Celia Kent who edited the book with skill and understanding. Finally my particular acknowledgement to the Egyptologists who have devoted their lives to deciphering the ancient inscriptions without whose work this book could not have been written.

Thanks are due to Yale University Press for permission to quote from *The Literature of Ancient Egypt, An Anthology of Stories, Instructions and Poetry* edited by W. K. Simpson and to Macdonald and Jane's to quote from *Island of Isis*.

THE WISDOM OF
THE ANCIENT EGYPTIANS

★

STORIES AND SAYINGS

THE WISDOM OF
THE ANCIENT EGYPTIANS

THE Ancient Egyptians gave the world the first major civilization in history. Like the Nile which cradled its growth, the surprising ideas of these remarkable people flowed out to the world around them. In this early period, some 6,000 years ago, two other civilizations were stirring: the Sumerian in the valleys of the Tigris and Euphrates, and the Chinese on the Yellow River. Of these, now only the Chinese remains but in antiquity neither the Chinese nor the Sumerians reached the level achieved by the people of the Nile Valley or affected Western civilization so much.

The Ancient Egyptians over whom the god-kings, the Pharaohs, ruled were a mixture of white skinned Libyans of North Africa—possibly of European descent—black skinned people from further south, such as the Somalis and Gallas, and various nomadic tribes of Semitic descent. They were united during the reign of King Menes, of the First Dynasty or family, who lived in 3100 B.C. This amalgamation of Africa and Europe, combined with the energy and mysticism of the wandering tribes from the East, produced a culture that laid the foundation for many aspects of our modern life: medicine, astrology, measurement, taxes, law, military strategy, writing, religion, poetry, music, painting, sculpting, drama, ritual and ceremony, mathematics, agriculture, irriga-

3

tion, ship building, the production of bows and arrows, nets and traps for fishing and hunting, spears and javelins for war, the breeding of ducks and geese, pigs, cattle, and even ibises for sacrifice to Imhotep.

Forty-five centuries ago their development of mathematics made possible the building of the Great Pyramids at Giza, but perhaps their most important contribution to the advance of civilization was the invention of paper, without which much of the world's literary heritage would have been lost. They had not, like the Babylonians, to press cuneiform signs into clay; they could write with pens on paper as we have learnt to do from them.

Papyrus rolls, the forerunner of books, existed for 3,000 years before they were superseded by the codex, an imitation of wax tablets held together with string. Some six centuries B.C., Greek literature was preserved on papyrus and before this it is likely that Hebrew literature was written on the same material. Certainly in later times the Torah was written on papyrus and has never lost the old roll form. It is fortunate for the world that the Egyptians discovered, about 3000 B.C., how to convert into paper the tall papyrus reeds that grew in such abundance. Today the reeds are not to be found north of the Sudan. Papyrus, often growing to a height of five metres, was also used to make boats, ropes, mats, boxes and sandals. Paper was made by cutting the thick stems into short pieces, stripping off the outside skin and cutting the pith into thin slices. The slices were then laid side by side, and another set was laid over them at right angles. By pressing and beating the two layers were welded together and dried under pressure. Finally the surface was smoothed with a polished stone and the sheets trimmed. The sheets were gummed together to form long scrolls of varying lengths according to the requirements of the scribes. Some of these magnificent manuscripts are over a hundred feet long. The scribes wrote on these scrolls with brushes made from a rush which still grows in Egypt; in later times thicker pens were made from reeds. The rush brush was dipped in black ink made from fine soot, probably from cooking pots, mixed with a thin solution of gum. Red ink was made by mixing finely ground red ochre with gum and water. Fortunately the colours were permanent. The rushes and the colours, in the form of dried cakes, were kept in the writer's palette and brush case together with a small pot filled with water for dissolving their colours. The scribe wrote first on the side that had the horizontal fibres uppermost, usually in vertical columns, beginning on the right and unrolling the scroll as he required more space. When he wished to write horizontally he limited the length of the line say to 20 cm. and made each additional line below it a similar length. When he reached the bottom of the page he would unroll the papyrus and leave a small margin before commencing the next page. Writing with a brush was more like painting. The hand did not touch the paper so that there was no danger of smudging. Wooden boards smoothed with gesso and painted white, like school slates, could be wiped clean and used again. For casual notes and jottings flakes of limestone and potsherds were used; these are now known as ostraca.

The peak of the Egyptian art of writing, as far as technique and beauty are concerned, is found in the best copies of the *Book of the Dead*. This book consists of series of spells which, when recited, generated magical power which was believed to make life easier for the dead. These books were frequently beautifully illustrated with pictures of the deceased with his wife and family in the underworld. Egyptian literature covers a wide variety of subjects: wisdom, meditation, poetry, hymns, magic, stories, travel, letters, business and legal records, science and astronomy.

The wisdom literature, of which many examples follow in the second part of this book, deals chiefly with 'Instructions' as their Egyptian title suggests. *The Instructions of Ptahhotep* were written by a vizier of the Pharaoh Djedkare Isesi (*c.* 2370 B.C.) who wished to make way for his son. He was told by the Pharaoh to instruct his son in the requirements of the office for 'no one is born wise'. The instruction begins with these words: 'Be not proud because thou art learned, be not over confident because thou art well-informed. Take counsel with the ignorant man as with the learned.'

These works were very popular and evidence of this is reflected in the fact that the *Instructions of Ammenemes I* is preserved in no fewer than four papyri, a leather roll, three wooden tablets and some fifty ostraca. What was it that produced the wisdom of this remarkable civilization and enabled it to continue with unbroken sway for some 3,000 years? To discover the answer we must go back to man's beginnings in this daunting area.

Just as wine takes its quality from minerals deep in the soil which feed the vine, and from the climate in which it grows, so did the early inhabitants of Egypt. At first they found themselves in damp, lush conditions where water and food were abundant, but this gradually gave way to drought. They had to adapt themselves to the forces of nature, or perish. The heat of the sun no longer shielded by luxuriant foliage, beat down on an arid world of sand and rock. The need for water became paramount. The distance between oases and water holes had to be accurately gauged, the position and direction calculated by the stars. Mistakes meant death. Overhead the burning sun rode across the vault of heaven dominating all living things until it sank in a blaze of glory in the sunset of the Western desert. As these early men sat in rude tents or sheltered in caves or clefts in the rocks, they were at the mercy of the natural forces around them; their survival depended upon their ability to overcome these hazards. It is unlikely that they realized that they were doomed to die of old age even if they succeeded in avoiding death from the many causes surrounding them. Today some aborigines of Australia do not believe in natural death and if they are not killed by some obvious accident such as drowning or being attacked by wild animals, they believe that their sickness in old age is caused by malevolent spirits. More advanced races also believe

7

that disease and death are the result of sin or the work of evil spirits. 'The wages of sin is death.'

Life was a continual struggle for the first people of Ancient Egypt. Death was constantly in their thoughts and the country supplied plenty of grim reminders. Hawks and vultures hovering over a stricken beast, corpses preserved, desiccated by the hot dry sand. The arid desert marched beside the living green pastures growing in the black soil brought by the flooding Nile. Everywhere man saw the contrast between life and death. He had solved some of the problems of survival, he begat children for the continuity of his race, but for all his skills he was doomed to die, death was inevitable unless he could find some solution that enabled him to overcome it.

In those early pre-dynastic days men lived by hunting. The animals and birds they pursued had qualities that were envied by the hunters and it was not difficult for them to worship the bird for flight, the wild bull for its strength, the ram for fertility and so on. Cave dwellings in France, Spain and Africa contain earlier evidence of the relationship between man and beast. They are drawn with great beauty on the walls of sacred caves where no doubt the qualities of the animals were transferred to man, or an ability to overcome them was achieved. Man eventually became master of his animal gods and required a god that had infinite power. The answer was at hand. It soared overhead, it prescribed his daily life, it gave him light and warmth, indeed sometimes too much. It divided his days, made the seasons and provided growth for his crops, but most important it arose afresh each morning after dying the night before. It demonstrated an order that had none of the frailties of his man-made world. So the sun became a god—endowed by man with fateful human qualities, qualities of mercy and of vengeance. For better or for worse, a religion was born.

The immediate result of the 'finding' of the god was the establishing of a new class of people whose skills were to serve the god and interpret his commandments to the tribe. This removed from them the burden of daily toil and gave them time to think and authority to further their ambitions. They wrote in hieroglyphs, picture writing, which enabled the writer to indicate the event he was writing about but often made it difficult for the reader to understand the message. Some words are impossible to draw but the Ancient Egyptians discovered a simple solution. They did, in fact, lay the foundation for the first alphabet and without this their intellectual life would have been unable to expand. An English illustration of their method might run as follows: a drawing of an 'eye' could have three meanings. An 'eye', 'to see', and the sound 'I'. Thus in a very simple form the picture of an eye repeated three times could mean, 'I see an eye'. The interpretation of the hieroglyphs baffled every investigator until in 1799 when a French officer serving in the Napoleonic army in Egypt discovered at Rosetta a large stone containing three similar texts, one in hieroglyphs, one in demotic (the script of the people) and the last in Greek and easily readable. In 1822 a

French orientalist, Jean-François Champollion, by comparing the royal names on the 'Rosetta Stone' was able to convince the world of the phonetic values of individual hieroglyphs, using the two names Ptolemy and Cleopatra to prove his theory. Following his discovery Egyptologists were then, in a remarkably short time, able to decipher the writings of the Ancient Egyptians, not only the inscriptions on the temples and tombs but also on the thousands of papyrus scrolls.

The priests, headed by the Pharaoh, the god-king, maintained their authority by developing obscure theologies involving a great diversity of gods. The old animal gods who were still popular were not discarded but were given human characteristics. The form usually taken was to place the animal head on the human body. This was done so artistically that even today the composite result seems both natural and attractive. Sometimes various aspects of the god or goddess are depicted. Hathor, the goddess of love, drinking and all the delights of the senses, is shown as a beautiful woman with the ears of a cow, or with the horns of a cow holding the sun's disc between them.

Egyptian logic demanded that life must have had a beginning and their concept of this is markedly similar to the account in the Bible. At first there was nothing but a wilderness of darkness and water. From this desolate waste emerged the god Atum, who came into existence by himself and produced a god Shu, who represented the air upon which all breathing creatures depend, and a goddess Tfenet, who represented the water which surrounded the earth and upon which it floated; when a well was dug the digger came upon this water. In addition to supplying air, Shu also had the task of holding up the sky. Geb and Nut finally produced Osiris, Isis, Seth and Nephthys. These gods formed the Ennead, the divine company of nine which later was also regarded as a single divine entity. From this the Ancient Egyptians conceived the universe as represented by the air-god Shu standing and supporting with his hands the outstretched body of the sky-goddess Nut, with Geb, the earth-god, lying at his feet.

The subjects of the Pharaoh were, like most modern Egyptians, an agricultural people. The old nomadic hunters had become farmers and the new communities were controlled by the inundation of the Nile. Each year all the land was flooded and each man's field had to be marked out anew when the waters subsided. This demanded great accuracy on which the peace of the community depended. In addition, the height of the Nile floods was measured on Nilometers, the higher the flood the greater the harvest and the more tax payable. During the four months of each year that the land was covered by the silt-bearing flood, the Egyptians took advantage of the situation to float barges of huge stones to various sites remote from the river banks. In this manner stones were transported to build the great pyramids and erect monuments. The only other method of transporting these huge stones overland was on heavy sledges pulled by hundreds of people over constantly replaced wooden rollers. We will deal later with their ingenious method of erecting the tall obelisks, some weighing a thousand tons. The Egyptians obviously took pleasure in this work; like the builders and masons of the Renaissance they must have felt enormous satisfaction in their magnificent achievements. No one seeing the pyramids for the first time can fail to be impressed. Originally they were even more spectacular, sheathed in white limestone, reflecting the radiance of the sun-god.

As soon as the floods subsided, the damp easily-worked soil was quickly brought into bearing. In the pictures on the walls of the tombs we see the seed scattered by hand from a sack tied round the sower's neck. Behind him came the ploughmen with his two small oxen yoked by a wooden halter to a primitive wooden plough. This was sufficiently strong to work the stoneless Nile silt and bury the seed. To keep the plough straight another man or a child led the oxen. Sometimes when the ground was sufficiently soft after its long immersion the farmer would scatter corn and then lead his flock of sheep or goats across it, to cover the seed. Gradually the soil dried out and the peasants now had to water their crops. The lucky ones were able to use irrigation canals bringing water from reservoirs at slightly higher levels filled during the flood. Others raised water by counterweighted scoops known as shadufs. Water wheels turned by animals, and Archimedes screws turned by hand, helped to bring the vital fluid to the level of the crops. The hardest method was carrying water pots up the steep river banks to fill the irrigation channels.

Eventually as the corn began to ripen the peasant was faced with his worst hazards. Apart from the natural enemies of drought, locusts, rats, birds and disease, he was now subjected to visitations by representatives of the tax authority with their following of surveyors, servants and scribes. The taxes went to the Treasury where the land was owned by the government or to the administrating priests if the land belonged to gods like Amun who owned the richest land in all Egypt. We see the surveyors in the tomb of Menna carrying the tools of their trade, writing palettes with pens and twin recesses for the black and red ink, balls of twine, stakes and the inevitable papyrus scrolls for the scribes. The first stake was driven in and the twine measured along the side of the field to a second stake and so on. Birds and inquisitive spectators are kept at bay whilst the peasants watch the officials reckoning their dues. It would be several weeks before the corn was out and threshed and the taxes paid. Meanwhile all the particulars were entered in the papyrus scrolls, red being used to emphasize the more important items.

The corn was cut not far below the head with a short handled sickle. The Egyptians used straw for making bricks out of the Nile mud—you cannot make bricks without straw. After cutting, the corn was carried by donkeys to the threshing floor, whilst women and children gleaners picked up anything that was left. The threshing floor was of beaten earth and when covered with a thick layer of corn oxen were driven on it and urged on by men who carried forks to turn over the crop. The oxen were not muzzled and snatched a mouthful here and there. As soon as the oxen had finished, the grain and chaff were roughly separated by forking and further divided by sweeping with brooms. Finally it was winnowed with flat scoops. The corn was then measured in bushels under the eyes of the ever-watchful scribes who already knew from their previous visit how much to expect. There was no mercy for the peasant who tried to keep part of his crop and even if he were honest but could not pay he was awarded the same treatment, stretched on the ground and methodically beaten.

Flax was another important crop. We see it pulled by hand in the tomb of Senedjem. It was then tied in bundles with the stalks pointing in both directions so that each end showed the small blue flowers. The Egyptians were experts in weaving and spun yarn so fine that mummy wrappings have been found with the incredible number of sixty-four threads in the warp and forty-eight in the weft per square centimetre. Many of the women's garments were of gauze-like fineness through which their figures could be clearly seen. Ancient Egyptian sculptors and painters depicted these delicate garments to perfection. Men's clothing was a loincloth but women wore a great many styles, some flowing, pleated gowns, sometimes leaving one breast exposed. Some dresses were narrow sheaths, occasionally covered with beads, impossible for the wearer to sit down. Necklines were of infinite variety: square, wedge-shaped, round, plunging to the waist or with a high collar round the neck. The wall paintings leave no doubt about the importance of dress and feminine allure for the Egyptian ladies.

Make up and jewellery were also of the greatest importance. Jars of unguents came in all shapes and sizes. Perfumes, spices and essences were in great demand against body odour. Body hair was considered unhygienic; priests were allowed to enter the temple only after the removal of all hair. Toe nails and finger nails were kept short. The Egyptians washed several times a day and also rinsed their mouths before and after meals. Great importance was attached to cleanliness. Where wealth permitted, clothes were changed several times a day as the climate demanded. Ceremonial wigs were worn by the ladies, framing the face and ending just short of the breasts. Serving girls' only clothing appeared to be a thin girdle of faience beads and children also went about naked. Dancing girls and female musicians appear on the wall paintings dressed largely in jewellery, but frequently wore diaphanous clothes. Nakedness did not seem to be of importance; the ladies made the most of their charms and covered them or uncovered them to their best advantage. Jewellery was universally worn, indeed the human need for jewellery has been in evidence from earliest times. The dwellers of the Nile valley were already wearing jewellery long before the Dynastic era. With the passage of time the prehistoric decorations of claws, teeth, shaped bones and rough stone beads gave way to more sophisticated bracelets and necklaces. Further refinements provided the astounding objects that have come from the tomb

15

of Tutankhamun. The Ancient Egyptians did not have diamonds or precious stones but they worked wonders with the semi-precious stones at their disposal. Amethyst, lapis-lazuli, turquoise, green feldspar, cornelian, rock-crystal and many colours in faience were skilfully worked by artist-craftsmen who moulded, fired, glazed and set the stones into gold, copper and bronze arm bands, rings, necklaces, bracelets, earrings, amulets and wide heavy collars that required counter-weights hanging down the wearer's back to balance the pull on the front. Some of the most popular forms showed the eye of Horus, and young married women wore the well-known fertility symbol of Isis giving her breast to her son Horus. In addition to jewellery, cloth head bands adorned with flower petals were worn for special occasions and on top of the head a perfumed cone of wax which scented the wearer as it gradually dissolved in the course of the evening.

Music was also part of Egyptian culture from earliest times. The flute, oldest of man's musical instruments, is shown in the tomb of Nakht where a girl musician plays a double flute accompanied by her two companions on a lute and a harp. Small hand drums, tambourines, hollowed-out wooden clappers, like castanets, supplied percussion. There were also hand rattles made of metal, called sistrums, but they were used for religious purposes and to intimidate the enemy in battle. One of the most attractive instruments was the harp; the large one standing on the ground had from eleven to fourteen strings and the smaller lyre half that number.

Many of the male harpers were blind and probably composed their own songs. The most famous is 'Song of the Harper'.

Rejoice and let thy heart forget that day when they shall lay thee to rest.

Cast all sorrow behind thee, and bethink thee of joy until there come that day of reaching port in the land that loveth silence.

Follow thy desire as long as thou livest, put myrrh on thy head, clothe thee in fine linen.

Set singing and music before thy face.

Increase yet more the delights which thou hast, and let not thy heart grow faint. Follow thine inclination and thy profit.

Do thy desires upon earth, and trouble not thine heart until that day of lamentation come to thee.

Spend a happy day and weary not thereof. Lo, none may take his goods with him, and none that hath gone may come again.

No form of musical notation has been found but efforts have been made to discover a scale from the position of the hands of the musicians but without success. Stringed instruments were plucked by hand, there is no evidence of the use of bows.

Dancing is depicted in many places but not between the sexes. Nor are men seen dancing together. A man may dance surrounded by a group of male spectators sometimes clapping, but no musicians appear in these pictures. Girls, on the other hand, danced singly and in groups; sometimes in religious processions and rituals, at others in the relaxed atmosphere of the banquets, naked and unashamed. 'Well nourished and of friendly heart.'

The images of the gods were treated as living persons and were washed, clothed and provided with food and servants. The people were encouraged not only to pay the priests but also to make gifts to the god so that they might receive favours in return. It was dangerous to refrain from making gifts as this could offend the god and lead to unpleasant retribution.

As we have seen, from humble beginnings and devotion to one god, there slowly arose a multiplicity of gods. The original idea expanded until each tribe and province provided themselves with their own particular deity. Life became more orderly, the fear of death was replaced by the hope of a future life, but worshippers were becoming inquisitive. What would the future be like, how would they get there, what indeed would they be like when they got there, would they be young again or as old as they were when they died? The priests provided answers to these perplexing questions.

The most important product of their reasoning was the Osiris myth. The legend relates that in remote antiquity Osiris ruled as king of Egypt in a humane manner, teaching men the rudiments of civilization and bringing prosperity to the country. His brother Seth was jealous of him and conspired to kill him. At a banquet he persuaded Osiris to enter a cunningly made chest, which Seth and his accomplices then closed and threw into the Nile. The river carried the chest down to the sea where it was washed ashore near the Syrian city of Byblos. Meanwhile, Isis, the distraught wife of Osiris, searched everywhere for her lost husband. At length she succeeded in discovering the chest which she took back to Egypt and there mourned over her husband in solitude. She then buried the body and went to see their son Horus, who was being brought up at Buto on the Nile. During her absence Seth, while engaged in a boar hunt, found the body and cut it up into fourteen pieces which he scattered throughout Egypt. As soon as Isis heard what had happened she set out to find the pieces. This she succeeded in doing and Re the sun-god sent down his son Anubis to wrap the body in bandages like those of a mummy. Isis caused breath to enter it and Osiris miraculously lived and moved again.

Osiris, unable to return as an earthly king, reigned in the spirit world as god of the dead. In this capacity he did not conflict with any of the established gods and no Egyptian whatever his local god or goddess might be, had any difficulty in also adopting Osiris and his creed. This was essentially that man after death lived again in the underworld, provided the proper rites had been observed. Every Ancient Egyptian firmly believed that because Osiris died and rose again to live in eternal blessedness he, too, could obtain the same destiny provided that the requirements of religion had been duly satisfied and that he had become one with Osiris. Osiris also appeared in other roles. He was one of the Nile-gods and with each inundation of the river he was believed to have risen again. He was also a god of fertility. Funeral trays carved in his shape were filled with earth and planted with corn which sprouted to life beside the mummy in the darkness of the tomb.

Isis his wife became the divine symbol of motherhood; she was also a mourning goddess, one of the four goddesses who protected the dead body. Her great cult centre in later times was her temple at Philae where she was worshipped with her husband Osiris and their son Horus.

Horus, who was originally a falcon-god and identified with the living king, was later also worshipped as one of a trinity with his father, Osiris, and mother, Isis. His eye is still regarded as a powerful protection in the Mediterranean where it is painted on the prows of fishing boats. Similar eyes are also seen on Chinese junks and the eye of Horus was worn as an amulet by the Ancient Egyptians. Horus, when he grew up, became transformed into the falcon-headed god of the heavens and received the name Re-Harakhty, 'the sun, the Horus who is on the horizon'. It is in this form that he is worshipped at the famous temples of Abu Simbel. Horus now set out to avenge his father's death and after many terrible contests with Seth was at last victorious. Gods, however, could not be killed, so Seth like Satan was able to continue his existence.

Just as Osiris after his death, was judged to see if he were a fit person to receive eternal life, so too was anyone who wished to share his immortal state. The judgement took place in a great hall where the dead person had to appear before forty-two terrible beings. These were the assessors of Osiris, who had become the supreme judge. In the hall stood a large balance on which the heart of the dead person was weighed against truth, represented by a feather, the symbol of Maet, the goddess of truth. Sometimes instead of a feather a statuette of the goddess herself wearing an ostrich feather in her hair was placed on the scale. Should the weighing go against the deceased, a frightful creature, Amemit, a combination of crocodile, leopard and hippopotamus, waited to devour his heart. In pictures of the scene in papyrus scrolls of the *Book of the Dead*, the balance is always shown in equilibrium, which presumably was the most favourable position for the dead person; the weight of the heart, the instigator of man's actions, being exactly equal to truth. As he came before each of the assessors the deceased had to state that he had not committed the sin for which that assessor had authority to judge. This statement is the famous 'Negative Confession' which embodies the moral code of the Ancient Egyptians. It consists of a series of denials such as: I have not killed, I have not spoken falsely, I have not given short measure, and so on. The deceased is finally led before Osiris, the chief judge, by Horus for the final judgement.

The multiplicity of gods and goddesses was constantly being increased. During conflicts and conquests and for various political expediences, gods of one place became involved with their opposite numbers in other areas so that many aspects of the same god appeared throughout the land. Although this produced a diversity of doctrine there was one belief that the whole population held with ever increasing conviction, and that was that life continued after death. Man had been fashioned by god in his own image. The ancient scribes wrote: 'Well tended are men, the cattle of god. He created heaven and earth according to their desire. He made the breath of life for their nostrils. They are his images and have come forth from his body.'

The following prayer shows the Egyptians love of life and material things. Ramesses IV, son of Ramesses III, the builder of the great temple of Medinet Habu, prayed to Osiris as follows:

And thou shalt give me health, life and old age, a long reign and strength to all my limbs; sight to my eyes, hearing to my ears and pleasure to my heart daily. And thou shall give me to eat to satiety, and thou shall give me drink to drunkenness, and thou shalt promote my seed to be kings in this country to eternity and for ever. And thou shalt make me content every day, thou shalt listen to my voice in whatever I shall say unto thee and grant me very high Nile floods to furnish thy offerings and to furnish the offerings of the gods and goddesses, the lords of the Northern and Southern Egypt, to preserve the sacred bulls, to preserve all the people of thy lands, their cattle and their trees which thy hand has made. For it is thou who hast made them all; thou canst not abandon them to pursue another design with them, for that would not be right.

Occasionally the Pharaohs made greater demands on the gods. To become a Pharaoh it was, in theory, essential that one should be the son of a Pharaoh and married to a princess of the royal line. Queen Hatshepsut (1503–1482 B.C.), like Cleopatra fifteen centuries later, had considerable difficulty in overcoming prejudice against a female Pharaoh, but with the help of the priests she was able to claim that she was not the natural daughter of her father Thuthmosis I, but that she was the daughter of the God Amun. Amenophis III, also of doubtful title, followed her example and in Luxor Temple, which he gave to the priests in reward for supporting his contention, we see his descent from the god Amun. What the priests approved the people did not question.

The priests who were in the highest ranks and also the highest state officials were exceptionally intelligent men. Through the gods they ruled the people and supported the Pharaohs. Their manipulation of a great diversity of gods was astute and their reward was great. Their temple at Karnak covered more than sixty acres and could easily accommodate ten European cathedrals. The sun-god Amun whose house it was, possessed in the Twentieth Dynasty, 81,000 slaves, 420,000 head of cattle, 690 acres of land, 83 ships, 46 temples, and an enormous annual income of gold, silver, copper, and precious stones, with food, drink, clothing and everything necessary for the well-being of his devoted servants in great abundance. Only on one occasion was the power of the priests challenged and an endeavour made to rationalize the complexities of Egyptian polytheism. This happened in the reign of Akhenaten who was the husband of the beautiful and famous Queen Nefertiti. Akhenaten decreed that instead of the multiple gods one supreme being alone would be worshipped. This god he claimed was Aten, the sun-disc, the sole source of life, light, warmth and abundance on earth. He built a new city at El Amarna, Akhetaten, 'The Horizon of Aten', as the centre for his new cult. However, the new religion was only accepted during his lifetime, and during the reign of Tutankhamun, thought by some to have been his son, a return to the old gods was brought about amid the general rejoicing of the people.

Of all the memorials left by this unparalleled revolution none is more remarkable than the hymns that this enlightened Pharaoh composed. They are inscribed on the walls of the tombs at El Amarna and one shows a notable similarity to the one hundred and fourth Psalm of the Hebrews.

Thou arisest beauteous in the horizon of heaven, O living Aten, beginner of life, when thou didst shine forth in the eastern horizon, and didst fill every land with thy beauty.

Thou art comely, great, sparkling, and high above every land, and thy rays enfold the lands to the limit of all that thou hast made, thou being the sun and thou reachest their limits and subjectest them to thy beloved son.

Being afar off, yet thy rays are upon the earth. Thou art in men's faces, yet thy movements are unseen. When thou settest in the western horizon, the earth is in darkness after the manner of death.

The earth grows bright, when thou hast arisen, shining as Aten in the daytime. Thou banishest darkness and bestowest thy rays. The Two Lands are in festival, awakened they stand on their feet, thou hast lifted them up. Their limbs are cleansed, clothes put on, and their hands are upraised in praise at thy glorious appearing. The entire land does its work. All cattle are at peace upon their pastures. Trees and pastures grow green. Birds taking flight from their nest, their wings give praise to thy spirit. All animals frisk upon their feet. All that flyeth or alighteth live when thou arisest for them. Ships fare north and likewise fare south. Every road is opened at thy appearing. The fish in the river leap before thy face. Thy rays are in the Great Green (the sea). Who causest the male fluid to grow in women and who makest the water in mankind; bringing to life the son in the body of his mother; soothing him by the cessation of his tears; nurse (already) in the body, who givest air to cause to live all whom thou makest, and he descendeth from the body to breathe on the day of his birth; thou openest his mouth fully and makest his sustenance. The chick in the egg speaketh in the shell; thou givest him air in it to make him live; thou hast made for him his completion so as to break it, even the egg, and he cometh forth from the egg to speak of his completion, and he walketh upon his two feet when he comes forth from it.

How manifold are thy works. They are mysterious in men's sight. Thou sole god, like to whom there is none other . . .

(Sir Alan Gardiner, *Egypt of the Pharaohs*)

For life to continue after death three things were essential: the ability to measure up to the requirements of the assessors, to have a body that was incorruptible, and a safe place where it could rest undisturbed until the day of resurrection. The bodies of the early inhabitants of Egypt were preserved by the desiccating properties of the hot, dry desert sand. Had the climate been damp such preservation would not have been possible and religion might have taken a different course. Without the body there could be no survival after death. In addition to a body, men were considered to have a 'Ba' and a 'Ka'. The 'Ba' resembled the western idea of a soul which lived on after death. It was originally conceived as a bird and later as a bird with a human head. It was believed that the spirit left the body at death and flew freely about, but could return to the body provided that it was preserved. The 'Ka' was presumbed to be a kind of guardian double of the body which was born at the same time and accompanied the body through life to protect it. The 'Ka' did not expire with the body at death but continued to live and care for the deceased in the future world. The preservation of the body was achieved by embalming. It is referred to in Genesis 50.2–3, where 'Joseph commanded his servants the physicians to embalm his father . . . and forty days were fulfilled . . . the days of those who are embalmed . . . and the Egyptians mourned him three score days and ten.'

It was believed that the technique of mummification enabled the corpse to rise from the dead and to live again; it was the key to eternal life and over the years became highly sophisticated. In its simplest form it was the removal of the water content of the body by drying, much as strips of meat or fish are dried today. This method was used up to the end of the last century to preserve cadavers in the Catacombs of Palermo; their lightened bodies may still be seen hanging on the walls, in some cases looking extremely life-like. The word 'mummy' comes from the Arabic word *mumiya* meaning a body preserved in bitumen, although bitumen was not generally used in the mummification processes.

As time went on the process of embalming became more complex, eventually occupying a period of seventy days (from death to burial) and producing almost permanent results. During the period of mummification the priests recited the necessary prayers and incantations which would ensure the dead man's safe journey to the next world, thanks to the example of Osiris. As the ceremony advanced sacred amulets were placed on the body, in particular a piece of leather inscribed with the eye of Horus was placed over the slit through which the internal organs were withdrawn. Finally when the curing was complete bandaging commenced. This began at the extremities. Fingers and toes were separately wrapped and frequently encased in stalls of gold or silver. The penis was wrapped in a state of erection. The dried, shrunken tissues were padded out to the original proportions with rolls of cloth and the body cavities stuffed with mud, sand and cloth. During the bandaging, prayers were intoned and various unguents were poured on the wrappings: myrrh, olive oil, wax and essences. The correct amounts were important, too much would eat away the flesh, too little fail to preserve. The mummy of Tutankhamun received too much and was partially destroyed.

Protection of the mummy was the chief consideration and at first this was done by burying it in a chamber at the bottom of a deep shaft. Surrounding the burial chamber were store rooms for food and furniture. Above the entrance was raised a mastaba, a rectangular mound containing false doors by which the deceased might leave and enter his eternal home. Realizing that mastabas or pyramids, however large, could not protect the mummy, but only make clear its whereabouts, the priests decided on another plan for royal burials. Far south in the Theban hills on the west bank of the Nile at Luxor they found an ideal site, a remote and arid valley devoid of life or people. Here, in the valley of the Kings, every Pharaoh of the New Kingdom with the exception of Akhenaten was buried. Long descending passages were cut into the limestone cliffs and provided with false passages, deep pits and heavy stone wedges that dropped into place after the mourners had left and all the ceremonies completed. It must have seemed to the diligent priests that their god-kings were finally secure, but it was not to be. Many people knew where the secret tombs were placed: the workmen who cut them out of the living rock, the funeral furnishers, the mourners and perhaps from time-to-time one of the priests may have been guilty. In every case the inner chambers have been reached usually by fresh tunnelling and the sacred mummy despoiled. The tomb of Tutankhamun was entered, but for some reason the robbers left the burial chamber intact and did not return.

It is from the wall paintings in the tombs of the nobles and court dignatories, and from the papyrus scrolls that were buried with them that we learn of the life of the people. Here are glowing pictures of the lives their occupants led on earth and the similar lives they hoped to lead in the next world. The homes of the Ancient Egyptians, their palaces, the houses of the wealthy and of the high officials, the humble dwellings of the poor, all have perished and it is only from the objects found in their tombs, the painting and inscriptions on their walls and in the temples that their way of life can be discovered.

Two tombs of considerable contrast are of particular interest, that of Tutankhamun because of its treasure (his innermost coffin alone, richly ornamented, was made of solid gold and weighed 210 kilos), and the humbler tomb of Paheri at El Kab. The former is world famous but the latter is unlikely to have been heard of by the general public. Paheri was a business-like countryman, a scribe of noble birth and trusted by the Pharaoh. His tomb is remarkable for its scenes of contemporary life and its lengthy inscriptions about them.

The El Kab lies fifty-two miles south of Luxor on the east bank and once ranked among the chief cities of Ancient Egypt and even in prehistoric times. The local goddess Nekhbet was represented either as a vulture or a woman wearing the crown of upper Egypt. She was a protecting deity and also helped women in childbirth. Like the tomb of Tutankhamun Paheri's tomb is small and cut into a rock cliff. It was built around 1500 B.C. and was discovered on 20 September 1799 during Napoleon's expedition. Here for the first time the subjects of the Pharaohs were revealed as living persons, a situation that has been repeated by many later discoveries. The tomb contains records of the Paheri family covering seven generations, going back to his great-great-grandmother and forward to his grandchildren. Paheri's chief function was 'Scribe of the accounts of corn' and in this office he was responsible to the Pharaoh as inspector of cornland over a large area. He was also the chief priest of Nekhbet, the goddess of Nekheb, the name of the city.

It is from tombs like this that the ideas and thoughts of the Ancient Egyptians are discovered and I am greatly indebted to the Egypt Exploration Society for publishing an examination of this tomb in 1894, from which these extracts are taken. Most of the inscriptions are in the form of prayers to the goddess, 'For the soul of Paheri' that he may receive various blessings including the offerings that are laid upon the altar. On the walls are scenes from daily life. Ploughmen behind their oxen sing, 'A fine day, one is cool, the oxen are drawing, heaven is doing according to our hearts, let us work for the noble'. A labourer sees Paheri watching and says, 'Friend, hasten at the work, let us finish in good time'. An overseer holding a stick says to two men carrying a huge basket of corn to the threshing-floor, 'Hasten ye, quicken your feet; the water is coming and will soon reach the baskets'. This refers to the Nile flood coming before the harvest is won. A man driving five oxen round the threshing floor sings, 'Thresh for yourselves, Oxen, thresh for yourselves; straw to eat, corn for your masters; let not your hearts be still; it is cool'.

The final inscription on the back wall of the tomb runs to more than fifty lines; the themes are the virtues of the deceased, prayers for a happy future and the desire that visitors should repeat the prayers to ensure ample food and drink for the spirit. The following passage gives some idea of the detail with which this careful scribe planned that his name and qualities would be safeguarded for posterity.

I am a departed soul that was good to his lord, wise of countenance, without failure of heart; I walked upon the road I had planned, I knew that which results from life; I reckoned the boundaries in writing. . . . All matters of the royal house, life, prosperity and health, were like the Nile flowing to the Great Green (the sea). My mouth was firm in improvement for my master; I feared for the matter of the balance, [was meticulous in his accounts]. I did not speak to deceive another. I knew the god who is in men.

It ends with the exhortation:

O ye living and existing nobles and people upon earth, servants of the gods and those connected with them, every scribe who takes the palette, skilful in divine words . . . and whosoever bends his hand in prayer may he act in the correct manner and perform his devotion in accordance to the rules, testifying from the reading of the command here written: 'mayest thou have loaves by the thousand, beer by the thousand and by the hundred thousand all things good sanctified by offering and pure for the Osiris . . . Paheri' . . . and finally, 'May your hearing of this be pleasant.'

This last is the concluding sentence in letters of the period, and not inappropriately ends this long address to visitors to the tomb of Paheri.

None of the dwellings of these Ancient Egyptians remain, but from the tombs we can reconstruct much of their way of life. The most important provider for the community was undoubtedly the farmer but he was regarded by the scribes as the lowest of all manual workers. He, poor chap, they said wore out as quickly as his tools. He had to face not only natural enemies such as rats, plagues of locusts, water shortages and scorching sandstorms, but he was often beaten and exploited by his master and by the tax collectors. His hard won harvest was robbed by thieves and his wife and children might be seized as security for debt. Notwithstanding all this, the toiler on the land was and still is a happy fellow. He frequently sings and we see pictures of him ploughing, reaping and enjoying the fruits of his labour.

Land and water were equally important to the town dweller and the ambition of every Egyptian was to have a garden where he might grow his own fruit and vegetables. Every garden had a few vines trained up poles to arches overhead with the clusters of black grapes hanging down. They were regarded as a great delicacy and in some of the tombs the ceilings are covered with painted bunches of this luscious fruit. Wine-making was also popular and in the tomb of Nakht the wall paintings show a group of young men treading grapes whilst they hold on to overhead ropes to keep them steady amongst the heady vapours. The wine was fermented in vats and stored in earthen amphorae sealed with plaster and marked according to quality.

A large part of the Nile valley was covered with marshes, stagnant lakes left by the receding floods, and this natural game reserve was the subject for many sculptors and painters who beautifully and realistically portrayed the scene. In the reeds and above them flocks of birds come and go. Here they nest and have their eggs and young stolen by wild cats and mongooses. The water below teems with fish including the great Nile perch, which required two men to lift it. The water also was a home for the hippopotamus and crocodile. Birds are trapped in nets or brought down with boomerangs ornamented with snakes' heads. Fish are caught on hook and line, harpooned, netted or caught in wicker traps. Even the huge hippopotamus is harpooned with heavy metal barb fixed in a wooden shaft and attached to a line buoyed with floats. The stricken beast makes off, breaking the wooden haft but unable to get rid of the imbedded harpoon. The hunters pull on the rope and when the animal turns to face them it is killed with spear thrusts. In the desert gazelles and antelopes are hunted by specially trained dogs and brought down with bows and arrows. Traps and nets are set up in narrow passes and game driven into them. Kings and nobles hunt from their chariots with bows and arrows.

The first houses were built of reed matting daubed with mud. Later this was replaced by sun-dried bricks made from Nile mud and sand bound with straw. The mud-brick houses were plastered inside and out and the plaster served as a base for lively and beautiful drawings and paintings of the life that went on around the owner. In 2850 B.C. the brilliant Imhotep constructed the first great building of dressed stone, the Step pyramid at Saqqara. The handling of immense blocks of stone was as highly skilled work as anything accomplished today. Obelisks weighing a thousand tons were separated from the mother granite by pounding a channel round the outline to the depth required. This channel had to be wide enough to allow the workers to cut slots in the underside with bronze chisels. Dry wooden wedges were then hammered into the slots and at night, when evaporation was least, they were soaked with water and the resulting swelling split the mass from its base. No wheeled vehicle could have supported these great weights and we see the stones dragged on massive sledges over wooden rollers by armies of men. Water is continually poured over the runners to make them slide more easily and as the sledge moves forward the logs passed over are rapidly laid in front and the process continues until the site is reached. Here the monument is dragged up a ramp and its base tipped into a prepared hole half filled with sand. By rope and tackle it is pulled upright and by removing the sand through a hole in the bottom of the ramp the monument is lowered gently until its settles in its final position. Many monuments were transported by river barges to places hundreds of miles from the quarries.

The might of the Egyptian Pharaohs lasted from King Menes, first Pharaoh of the first Dynasty c. 3100 B.C., until Alexander the Great conquered the country in 332 B.C. After his death in 323 B.C. his generals divided the kingdoms he had conquered between them. Egypt was taken over by Ptolemy, a fine statesman and one of Alexander's most trusted generals. He was welcomed by the Egyptians as a Pharaoh who had delivered them from Persian domination and he took the title Soter I, Saviour. There were fifteen Ptolemies altogether and the last was Caesarion, Little Caesar, Cleopatra's son by Julius Caesar. He was murdered in 30 B.C. whilst fleeing from Octavian's forces, and for Cleopatra his death ended the Dynasty and now nothing remained but the prospect of appearing in chains at a Roman triumph. She decided to take her life. Serpents have always been part of the royal insignia of the Pharaohs and the legend may be true that she allowed herself to be bitten by a snake. When Octavian's men came for her they found her lying on a golden couch in her royal robes. She was already dead. Her servant Charmion was adjusting the diadem on the brow of her mistress. One of the guards called out 'Is this right?' and Charmion gave the final epitaph of the Dynasty: 'It is entirely right and fitting for a queen descended from so many kings'. Thus ended the 3,000 year rule of the Pharaohs, and Egypt came under direct rule from Rome.

The priests and gods of Ancient Egypt were also coming to the end of their long reign, but it was not the decrees of emperors so much as the new religion of Christianity that brought about their downfall. The Holy Family took refuge in Egypt after fleeing from Herod and it is reputed that they found shelter in the crypt of the church of St Sergius in Cairo during the Roman occupation. The altar in the crypt is still an object of reverence and its white marble is covered with the names of visitors, many of them Muslims, who still pay their respects. Nearby is the holy well at Mataria where the Virgin is reputed to have washed the Infant's clothes. In A.D. 62 St Mark was martyred by the Romans for protesting against the worship of Sarapis. The Emperor Hadrian is reputed to have written, 'Their one god is nothing peculiar', but he was proved to be wrong. The refusal of the Christians to admit that the emperor was god resulted in some 140,000 believers perishing for the cause, but this appalling persecution defeated itself and in A.D. 331 Constantine recognized Christianity as the official religion.

In the reign of Theodosius the Great (A.D. 379–95) Christianity was declared to be the religion of the entire Empire. The statues of the ancient gods and the temples of Egypt were enthusiastically destroyed by intolerant Copts. The old rites and writing were forbidden and the hieroglyphs soon became meaningless to the early Christians. Only the cult of Isis continued when the other gods and goddesses of antiquity had been forgotten. Pilgrims from Greece and the Roman Empire continued to worship her, heaping her shrine at Philae with offerings as late as the fifth century A.D. Her hymn states:

> I am the mother of all nature, mistress of all the elements, origin and principle of the centuries, supreme divinity, queen of the spirits, first among the inhabitants of the sky, unique among the gods and goddesses; the luminous summits of the sky, the salutary breezes of the sea, the desolate silences of hell, it is I who govern all at my will.

Finally in A.D. 577 her temple was converted into a Christian Church and Byzantine crosses were engraved on the walls and pillars amongst the reliefs of Isis, Osiris and Horus.

This was the end of the Pharaohs and people of Ancient Egypt but their contribution to civilization will remain as long as words are written. As the scribe sayeth:

> 'To speak of the Dead is to make them live again.'

STORIES AND SAYINGS

* I *

THE WORDS which man says are one thing, the
things which God doeth are another.

* II *

AMENEMOPE instructed:

Do not fraternize with the hot-tempered man,
    Nor approach him to converse.
Safeguard your tongue from answering your superior,
    And take care not to speak against him.
Do not allow him to stop talking only to entrap you,
    And be not too free in your replies;
With a man of your own station discuss the reply;
    And take care of speaking thoughtlessly;
When the heart is upset, words travel faster
    Than wind before water.

He ruins and creates with his tongue,
    And he speaks slander;
He makes an answer deserving of a beating,
    For its work is evil;
He sails among all the world,
    But his cargo is false words;
He acts the ferryman in knitting words:
    He goes forth and comes back arguing.

    For he sets families to argue.
He goes before all the winds like clouds,
    He diminishes his character in the sun;

He crooks his tail like a baby crocodile,
  He curls himself up as if injured;
His lips are sweet, but his tongue is bitter,
  And flame burns inside him.

Do not fly up to join that man
  Not fearing you will be brought to account.

★ III ★

MERIKARE was taught: Do justice, that you may live
long upon earth. Calm the weeper, do not oppress
the widow, do not oust a man from his father's
property, do not degrade magnates from their seats.
Beware of punishing wrongfully; do not kill, for it
will not profit you, but punish with beatings and with
imprisonment, for thus this land will be set in order,
excepting only the rebel who has conspired, for God
knows those who are disaffected, and God will smite
down his evil doing with blood.

★ IV ★

AN EGYPTIAN maid sang to her lover: There are
saamu-flowers in it. One is uplifted in their presence.
I am thy first sister. I am unto thee like the acre which
I have planted with flowers and all manner of sweet-
smelling herbs; and in it is a pool which thy hand hath
digged, in the cool of the north wind, a lovely place
where I walk, thine hand upon mine, and my body
satisfied and my heart glad at our going together. It is
mead to me to hear thy voice, and I live because I hear
it. If I but see thee it is better to me than eating and
drinking.

★ V ★

PTAHHOTEP said: If thou art a leader and command multitudes, strive after every excellence, until there be no fault in thy nature. Truth is good and its worth is lasting, it has not been altered since the day of its creator, whereas he that transgresseth its ordinances is punished. It lieth as a path in front of him that knoweth nothing. Wrong-doing hath never yet brought its venture to port. Evil indeed winneth wealth, but the strength of truth is that it endureth, and is the property of God.

★ VI ★

PTAHHOTEP said: Think much, but keep thy mouth closed; if thou dost not how canst thou consult with the nobles? Let thy opinion coincide with that of thy lord. Do what he saith, and then he shall say of thee to those who are listening: This is my son.

★ VII ★

THE MAXIMS OF ANI say: The heart of a man is like the store chamber of a granary that is full of answers of every kind; choose thou those that are good, and utter them, and keep those that are bad closely confided within thee.

★ VIII ★

ONCHSHESHONQY said: Do not do evil to a man and so cause another to do it to you. Do not be hard-hearted towards a man if you can intercede for him.

41

AMENEMOPE instructed:

Do not jeer at a blind man nor tease a dwarf,
　Neither interfere with the condition of a cripple;
Do not taunt a man who is in the hand of God,
　Nor scowl at him if he errs.

Man is clay and straw,
　And God is his potter;
He overthrows and he builds daily,
　He impoverishes a thousand if he wishes.
He makes a thousand into examiners,
　When he is in his hour of life.
How fortunate is he who reaches the West,
　When he is safe in the hand of God.

★ X ★

MERIKARE was taught by his father: The kingship is a goodly office; it has no son and it has no brother who shall make its monuments endure, yet it is the one person who ennobles the other; a man works for his predecessor, through the desire that what he has done may be embellished by another who shall come after him.

★ XI ★

THE MAXIMS OF ANI say: The man who uttereth ill-natured words must not expect to receive good-natured deeds.

★ XII ★

ONCHSHESHONQY advised: Enjoy your youth; the holiday is short; there is no man who does not die.

THE MAXIMS OF ANI say: The opportunity having passed, one seeketh in vain to seize another.

★ XIV ★

THE SCRIBE extols his own profession in the *Book of the Dead*: I am told that you have abandoned writing and taken to sport, that you have set your face towards work in the fields and turned your back upon letters. Remember you not the condition of the cultivator faced with the registering of the harvest-tax, when the snake has carried off half of the corn and the hippopotamus has devoured the rest? The mice abound in the fields. The locusts descend. The cattle devour. The sparrows bring disaster upon the cultivator. The remainder that is on the threshing-floor is at an end, it falls to the thieves. The yoke of oxen has died whilst threshing and ploughing. And now the scribe lands on the river bank and is about to register the harvest tax. The janitors carry staves and the Nubians rods of palm, and they say, 'Hand over the corn' though there is none. The cultivator is beaten all over, he is bound and thrown into the well, soused and dipped head downwards. His wife has been bound in his presence, his children are in fetters. His neighbours abandon them and are fled. So their corn flies away. But the scribe is ahead of everyone. He who works in writing is not taxed, he has no dues to pay. Mark it well.

★ XV ★

KING MERIKARE said to his son: The judges who judge the oppressed, thou knowest that they are not lenient on that day of judging the miserable, in the hour of carrying out the decision. Ill fareth it when the accuser is the Wise One! Put not thy trust in length of years; they regard a lifetime as an hour. A man remaineth after death and his deeds are placed beside him. But it is for eternity that one is there, and he is a fool that maketh light of them. But he that cometh unto them without wrong-doing, he shall continue yonder like a god, stepping boldly forward like the Lords of Eternity.

★ XVI ★

ONCHSHESHONQY taught:

Do not instruct a fool, lest he hate you.

Do not instruct him who will not listen to you.

Do not consult a wise man in a small matter when a large matter is to hand.

Do not consult a fool in a large matter when there is a wise man whom you can consult.

Do not laugh at instruction.

★ XVII ★

AMENEMOPE taught:

Do not address your intemperate friend in your un-righteousness,
   Nor destroy your own mind;
Do not say to him, 'May you be praised,' not meaning it
   When there is fear within you.
Do not converse with false men,
   For it is the abomination of God.

44

Do not separate your mind from your tongue,
   All your plans will succeed.
You will be important before others,
   While you will be secure in the hand of God.
God hates the falsification of words,
   His great abomination is duplicity.

★ XVIII ★

HIS FATHER taught Merikare: Wretched is he who has
bound the land to himself; a fool is he who is greedy
when others possess. Life on earth passes away, it is
not long; he is fortunate who has a good remembrance
in it.

★ XIX ★

ONCHSHESHONQY also taught: When you fare well, do
not be anxious lest you fare badly.

★ XX ★

KAGEMNI said: Be not boastful of thy strength in the
midst of those of thine own age. Be on thy guard
against any withstanding thee. One knoweth not what
may chance, what God doeth when he punisheth.

★ XXI ★

ONCHSHESHONQY wrote to his son: The blessing of a
craftsman is his tools.

★ XXII ★

ONCHSHESHONQY also said: Do not swear falsely when
you are in trouble lest you become worse off than you
are at present.

XXIII

AMENEMOPE instructed:

Do not get into a quarrel with the argumentative man
    Nor incite him with words;
Proceed cautiously before an opponent,
    And give way to an adversary;
Sleep on it before speaking,
    For a storm comes forth like fire in hay.
The hot-headed man in his appointed time:
    May you be restrained before him;
Leave him to himself,
    And God will know how to answer him.

If you spend your life with these things in your heart,
    Your children shall behold them.

XXIV

HE ALSO said:

Do not castigate your companion in a dispute,
    And do not let him say his innermost thoughts;
Do not fly up to greet him
    When you do not see how he acts.
May you first comprehend his accusation
    And cool down your opponent.

Leave it to him and he will empty his soul;
    Sleep knows how to find him out;
Take his feet, do not bother him;
    Fear him, do not underestimate him.
Indeed, you cannot know the plans of God,
    You cannot perceive tomorrow.

Sit yourself at the hands of God;
  Your tranquillity will annihilate them.

★ XXV ★

THE MAXIMS OF ANI say: The ruin of a man resteth on his tongue; take heed that thou harmest not thyself.

★ XXVI ★

ONCHSHESHONQY warned: There is none who plays a trick and who is not himself tricked. There is none who goes astray and then goes and prospers.

★ XXVII ★

ONCHSHESHONQY said: A man's personality is his strength. A man's personality is in his face.

★ XXVIII ★

THE MAXIMS OF ANI say: What ought people to talk about every day? Administrators of high rank should discuss the laws, women should talk about their husbands, and every man should speak his own affairs.

★ XXIX ★

KING MERIKARE said to his son: Be a craftsman in speech, so that thou mayest prevail, for the power of a man is the tongue, and speech is mightier than any fighting. He that is clever, him the learned attack not, if he is learned, and no harm happeneth where he is. Truth cometh to him fully kneaded, after the manner of that which the forefathers spake. Copy thy fathers, them that have gone before thee. Behold, their words

endure in writing. Open the book and read, and copy
the knowledge, so that the craftsman too may become
a wise man.

THE MAXIMS OF ANI say: Never speak an ill-natured
word to any visitor; a word dropped some day when
thou art gossiping may overturn thy house.

THE HEART and tongue have power over all members,
considering that the heart is in every body and the
tongue in every mouth of all gods, all men, all cattle,
all worms and all living beings, while the heart con-
ceives thoughts and the tongue commands freely. The
seeing of the eyes, the hearing of the ears and the
breathing of the nose report to the heart. And it is the
heart which produces all the cognition and it is the
tongue which repeats that which has been thought
out by the heart. And in this way is produced any
work and any craft, the activity of the arms, the walk-
ing of the feet, the movement of all members according to the order which has been thought out by the
heart, has come forth through the tongue and put into
effect with a view of accomplishing all things.

AMENEMOPE taught:
The hot-headed man in the temple
    Is like a tree grown outdoors;
Suddenly it loses its branches,
    And it reaches its end in the carpentry shop;

48

It is floated away far from its place,
   Or fire is its funeral pyre.

The truly temperate man sets himself apart,
   He is like a tree grown in sandy soil,
But it flourishes, it doubles its yield,
   It stands before its owner;
Its fruit is something sweet, its shade is pleasant,
   And it reaches its end in a garden.

★XXXIII★

THE MAXIMS OF ANI say: Answer not a man when he is wroth, but remove thyself from him. Speak gently to him that hath spoken in anger, for soft words are the medicine for his heart.

★XXXIV★

THE MAXIMS OF ANI say: Seek silence for thyself.

★XXXV★

ONCHSHESHONQY advised: Dumbness is better than a hasty tongue.

★XXXVI★

PTAHHOTEP said: If thou art one of a company seated to eat in the house of a man who is greater than thyself, take what he giveth thee. Set it before thee. Look at what is before thee, but not too closely, and do not look at it too often. The man who rejecteth it is an ill-mannered person. Do not speak to interrupt when he is speaking, for one knoweth not when he may disapprove. Speak when he addresseth thee, and then thy words shall be acceptable. When a man hath wealth he ordereth his actions according to his own dictates. He doeth what he willeth. The great man can effect by the mere lifting up of his hand what a humble man cannot. Since the eating of bread is according to the dispensation of God, a man cannot object thereto.

⋆ XXXVII ⋆

ONCHSHESHONQY warned: He who hides behind his master shall get five hundred masters.

⋆ XXXVIII ⋆

THE MAXIMS OF ANI say: Remain not seated whilst another is standing, especially if he be an old man, even though thy rank be higher than his.

⋆ XXXIX ⋆

ONCHSHESHONQY taught his son:

Do not long for your home when you are working.
Do not long for your home, to drink beer in it at mid-day.
Do not pamper your body, lest you become slack.
Do not pamper yourself when you are young, lest you become slack when you are grown-up.
Do not dislike a man on sight if you do not know anything about him.
Do not be distressed so long as you have something.
Do not be worried so long as you have something.
Do not be put out by things.
Do not be dissatisfied with your occupation.

★ XL ★

ONCHSHESHONQY wrote from his prison: Enquire about everything that you may understand it. Be good-tempered and magnanimous, that your disposition may be attractive.

★ XLI ★

THE MAXIMS OF ANI say: If thou art well-versed in books, and hast gone into them, set them in thy heart; whatsoever thou then utterest will be good. If the scribe be appointed to any position, he will converse about his documents. The director of the treasury hath no son, and the overseer of the seal hath no heir. High officials esteem the scribe, whose hand is his position of honour, which they do not give to children.

★ XLII ★

PTAHHOTEP said: Be not haughty because of thy knowledge. Converse with ignorant man was well as with him that is educated.

★ XLIII ★

ONCHSHESHONQY taught:

Serve your God that he may protect you.

Serve your brothers, that you may have a good reputation.

Serve a wise man, that he may serve you.

Serve him who serves you.

Serve any man in order to find profit.

Serve your father and your mother, that you may go and prosper.

★ XLIV ★

ANI wrote: Go not in and out in the court of justice, that thy name may not stink. Speak not much, be silent, that thou mayest be happy. Be not a gossip.

★ XLV ★

ANI also wrote: Keep thyself far from an hostile man, and take him not to thee for a companion. Make to thyself a friend of one that is upright and righteous.

★ XLVI ★

ONCHSHESHONQY taught: If you keep company with a man and are on good terms with him, do not leave him when he fares badly; let him attain his house of eternity; his heir will make provision for you.

★ XLVII ★

THE MAXIMS OF ANI say: Go not with common men, lest thy name may suffer.

★ XLVIII ★

PTAHHOTEP said: If thou desirest thy conduct to be good, to set thyself free from all that is evil, then beware of covetousness, which is a malady, diseaseful, incurable. Intimacy with it is impossible; it maketh the sweet friend bitter, it alienateth the trusted one from the master, it maketh bad both father and mother, together with the brothers of the mother, and it divorceth a man's wife. It is a bundle of every kind of evil, and a bag of everything that is blameworthy. Long lived is the man whose rule of conduct is right, and who goeth in accordance with his course; he winneth wealth thereby, but the covetous hath no tomb.

★ XLIX ★

ONCHSHESHONQY taught his son: Do not make yourself too offensive, lest you be insulted. The little man who behaves arrogantly is greatly detested. The great man who behaves modestly is highly respected.

★ L ★

PTAHHOTEP said: If thou dost humble thyself and dost obey a wise man, thy behaviour will be held to be good before God. Since thou knowest who are to serve, and who are to command, let not thy heart magnify itself against the latter. Since thou knowest who hath the power, hold in fear him that hath it.

★ LI ★

THE MAXIMS OF ANI say: When an inquiry is held, and thou art present, multiply not speech; thou wilt do better if thou holdest thy peace. Act not the part of the chatterer.

★ LII ★

THE MAXIMS OF ANI say: If thou journey on a road made by thy hands each day, thou wilt arrive at the place where thou wouldst be.

53

★ LIII ★

ONCHSHESHONQY taught: Do not run round in circles simply in order not to stand still, and: Do not run away after you have been beaten, lest your punishment be doubled, and: He who is stout-hearted in a misfortune shall not feel its full force.

★ LIV ★

ANI's writing advised: Guard thyself against ought that injureth great people, by talking of secret affairs. If anyone speaketh thus in thine house, make thyself deaf.

★ LV ★

THE MAXIMS OF ANI say: When the messenger of death cometh to carry thee away, let him find thee prepared. Alas, thou wilt have no opportunity for speech, for verily his terror will be before thee. Say not: Thou art carrying me off in my youth. Thou knowest not when death will take place. Death cometh, and he seizeth the babe at the breast of his mother, as well as the man who hath arrived at a ripe old age. Do these things, and thou wilt be a good man, and evils of all kinds shall remove themselves from thee.

★ LVI ★

PTAHHOTEP said: Thou canst obtain nothing in life by bluster; what hath come to pass is the command of God.

PTAHHOTEP said: Do not terrify the people, for if thou dost, God will punish thee. If any man saith that he is going to live by these means, God will make his mouth empty of food. If a man saith that he is going to make himself powerful thereby, saying: I shall reap advantage, having knowledge; and if he saith: I will beat down the other man; he will be able to do nothing. Let no man terrify the people, for the command of God is that they shall enjoy rest.

THIS *Hymn to Aten* was the first truly monotheistic composition in the literature of the world: When thou risest in the morning and shinest as Aten by day thou dost put to flight the darkness and givest forth thy rays. The Two Lands rejoice, they awake and stand on their feet, for thou hast aroused them. They wash their limbs and take up their clothes, their arms do adoration to thy rising. All the land performs its labours. All cattle rejoice in their pastures. The treees and herbs grow green. Birds and winged things come forth from their nests, their wings doing adoration to thy spirit. All goats skip on their feet, all that flies takes wing; they begin to live when thou risest on them. Ships ply upstream and downstream likewise; every path is opened by reason of thy rising. The fish in the stream leap before thy face, thy beams are in the depths of the ocean. Creator of issue in women, maker of seed in mankind, who quickenest the son in the womb of his mother, soothing him that he may not weep, nurse within the womb, who givest breath to quicken all whom he would create. When he comes forth from the womb on the day of his birth thou dost open his mouth and dost provide for his needs. When the chick in the egg cries within the shell thou givest him breath within it to quicken him; thou hast made for him his strength to break from within the egg. When he comes forth from the egg to chirp with all his might he goes upon his two legs when he comes forth from it.

How manifold are thy works! They are concealed from us. O sole god to whom no other is like! Thou didst create the earth according to thy desire when thou wast alone, men and cattle, all goats, and all that is upon the earth and goeth upon its feet, and all that is in the sky and flieth with its wings. The foreign lands too, Syria and Ethiopia, and the land of Egypt. Thou puttest each man in his place, thou providest for his needs, each one having his sustenance and his days reckoned. Their tongues are distinguished in speech; their characters likewise and their complexions are different. Thou hast distinguished the nations.

Thou createst the Nile in the Underworld and bringest it forth according to thy will to give life to mankind, even as thou didst create them for thyself, lord of all of them, who art weary by reason of them, lord of every land, who risest for them, Disk of the day, great of might. Thou art in my heart. There is none other that knoweth thee save thy son Akhenaten. Thou didst grant him to understand thy counsels and thy might when the earth came into being in thy hand;

even as thou didst make them. When thou risest they live, when thou settest they die. Thou art length of days in thyself. In thee men live. Eyes are on thy beauty until thou settest. All labour is set aside when thou settest in the west: but when thou risest work for the king is made to proceed apace. All men that run upon their feet since thou didst found the earth thou hast raised them up for thy son who came forth from thyself, even Akhenaten.

* LIX *

A HYMN to King Sesostris III:

How great is the lord of his city; he is a sanctuary that saves him who fears from his enemy.
How great is the lord of his city; he is a cool and refreshing shade in summer.
How great is the lord of his city; he is a corner warm and dry in wintertime.
How great is the lord of his city; he is like a mountain that wards off the blast when heaven rages.

* LX *

KING MERIKARE wrote: More acceptable to God is the virtue of one that is just of heart than the ox of him that doeth iniquity. Do something for God, that he may do the like for thee with an offering that replenisheth the offering-table, and with an inscription, one that perpetuateth thy name. God is cognizant of him that doeth something for him.

THE MAXIMS OF ANI say: When thou offerest up offerings to thy God, beware lest thou offer the things that are an abomination. Chatter not during his processions, seek not to prolong his appearance, disturb not those who carry him, chant not his offices too loudly, and beware lest thou let thine eye observe his dispensations. Devote thyself to the adoration of his name. It is he who giveth souls to millions of forms, and he magnifieth the man who magnifieth him.

THE MAXIMS OF ANI say: The sanctuary of God abhorreth noisy demonstrations. Pray thou with a loving heart, and let thy words be hidden. Do this, and he will do thy business for thee. He will hearken unto thy words, and he will receive thy offerings.

THE MAXIMS OF ANI say: Celebrate thou the festival of thy God, and repeat the celebration thereof in its appointed season. God is wroth with the transgressor of this law. Bear testimony to him after the offering.

AMENEMOPE said:

Do not go to bed fearing tomorrow,
    For when day breaks what is tomorrow like?
Man knows not how tomorrow will be!
God is success,
    Man is failure.

The words which men say pass on one side,
　The things which God does pass on another side.

Do not say, I am without fault,
　Nor try to seek out trouble.
Fault is the business of God,
　It is locked up with his seal.
There is no success in the hand of God,
　Nor is there failure before him;
If he turn himself about to seek out success,
　In a moment he destroys it.

Be strong in your heart, make your mind firm,
　Do not steer with your tongue;
The tongue of a man is the steering oar of a boat,
　And the Lord of All is its pilot.

★ LXV ★

MERIKARE's father said to him: Well tended are men,
the cattle of God. He made heaven and earth according to their desire. He allayed the thirst for water. He
made the air that their nostrils may live. They ariseth
in heaven according to their desire. He made for them
plants and cattle, fowls and fishes, in order to nourish
them. But he also punisheth: He slew his enemies, and
punished his children, because of that which they
devised when they were hostile.

★ LXVI ★

KING AKHTOY ordained in a teaching: Be inactive
about the violent man who destroys altars, for God
will attack him who rebels against the temples.

THE MAXIMS OF ANI say: Celebrate the feast of thy god. God is wroth with him that disregardeth it. Let witnesses stand by thine offering; it is best for him that hath done it. Singing, dancing and frankincense appertain to his maintenance, and the receiving of reverence appertaineth to his possessions. Bestow them on the god in order to magnify his name.

THE MAXIMS OF ANI say: God will magnify the name of the man who exalteth his Souls, who singeth his praises, and boweth before him, who offereth incense, and doeth homage to him in his work.

KING MERIKARE said: Exalt not the son of one of high degree more than him that is of lowly birth, but take to thyself a man because of his actions. Practise every craft, protect thy boundary and command thy fortresses, that the troops may be of service to their master. Make monuments for the god; they cause the name of their builder to live again. A man should do that which profiteth his soul: in that he performeth the monthly service of priest, putteth on white sandals, frequenteth the temple, uncovereth the mysteries, entereth the sanctuary, and eateth bread in the temple.

THE MAXIMS OF ANI say: Devote thyself to God, take heed to thyself daily for the sake of God, and let tomorrow be as today. Work thou for him. God seeth him that worketh for him, and he esteemeth lightly the man who esteemeth him lightly.

★ LXXI ★

KING MERIKARE said: Be not evil, it is good to be kindly. Cause thy monument to endure through the love of thee. Then men thank God on thine account, men praise thy goodness and pray for thine health.

Honour the great and prosper thy people; good is it to work for the future. But keep thine eyes open, one that is trusting will become one that is afflicted.

★ LXXII ★

ONCHSHESHONQY said: Do not be weary of crying to God, for he has his hour for hearing the scribe.

★ LXXIII ★

PTAHHOTEP said: If thou art a wise man, and if thou hast a seat in the council chamber of thy lord, concentrate thy mind on the business so as to arrive at a wise decision. Keep silence, for this is better than to talk overmuch. When thou speakest thou must know what can be urged against thy words. To speak in the council chamber needeth skill and experience.

★ LXXIV ★

PTAHHOTEP said: If thou has become a great man having once been a poor man, and hast attained to the headship of the city, study not to take the fullest advantage of thy situation. Be not harsh in respect of the grain, for thou art only an overseer of the food of God.

★ LXXV ★

ONCHSHESHONQY gave the following maxims about property:

Do not set your heart on the property of another,
    saying, I will live thereon; acquire property yourself.
When you have reached your prime and acquired
    much property let your brother share your wealth.
Every man acquires property; it is the wise man who
    conserves it.
Do not covet another's property, that you may not
    be in want yourself.
Do not trespass on the territory of another.
Do not build a house on agricultural land.

★ LXXVI ★

AMENEMOPE said:

Do not set your heart upon seeking riches,
    For there is no one who can ignore Destiny and
        Fortune;
Do not set your thoughts on external matters:
    For every man there is his appointed time.

Do not exert yourself to seek out excess
    So that your wealth will prosper for you;
If riches come to you by theft
    They will not spend the night with you;
As soon as day breaks they will not be in your house-
    hold;
    Although their places can be seen, they are not there.

When the earth opens up its mouth, it reckons him and
    swallows him up,
    And it drowns them in the deep;
They have made for themselves a great slit in their
    measure,
    And they have sunk themselves in the tomb;
Or they have made themselves wings like geese,
    And they fly up to the sky.
Do not be pleased with yourself because of riches
    acquired through robbery,
    Neither complain about poverty.
If an officer commands one who goes in front of him,
    His company leaves him;
    The boat of the covetous is abandoned in the mud,
    While the skiff of the truly temperate man sails on.
When he rises you shall offer to the Aten,
    Saying, Grant me prosperity and health.
And he will give you your necessities for life,
    And you will be safe from fear.

★ LXXVII ★

KING MERIKARE was taught: Make your magnates
great, that they may execute your laws; one who is
rich in his house will not be one-sided, for he who
does not lack is an owner of property; a poor man
does not speak truly, and one who says: 'Would that
I had,' is not straightforward; he is one-sided toward
the possessor of rewards. Great is the great one whose
great ones are great; valiant is a king who owns an
entourage; and august is he who is rich in magnates.
Speak truth in your house, so that the magnates who

are on earth may respect you, for a sovereign's renown lies in straightforwardness; it is the front room of a house that inspires the back room with respect.

PTAHHOTEP said: If thou art a man whose duty it is to enter into the presence of a nobleman with a message from another nobleman, take care to say correctly and in the correct way what thou art sent to say; give the message exactly as he said it. He who wresteth the truth in transmitting the message, and only repeateth it in words that give pleasure to all men, gentleman or common man, is an abominable person.

PTAHHOTEP said: If thou art a farmer, till the field which the great God hath given thee. Eat not too much when thou art near thy neighbours. The children of the man who, being a man of substance, seizeth prey like the crocodile in the presence of the field labourers, are cursed because of his behaviour, his father suffereth poignant grief, and as for the mother who bore him, every other woman is happier than she. A man who is the leader of a tribe that trusteth him and followeth him becometh a god.

ONCHSHESHONQY said about wealth:

In fair weather or foul, wealth increases by making the most of it. Good fortune will not happen to you; good fortune is given to him who seeks it.

Do not be mean; wealth is no security.
Wealth takes charge of its owner.

⋆ LXXXI ⋆

PTAHHOTEP said: If thou be grown great, after that
thou wast of small account, and have gotten thee
substance, after that thou wast aforetime needy in the
city which thou knowest, forget not how it fared with
thee in time past. Trust not in thy riches, that have
accrued to thee as a gift of God. Thou are not better
than another that is thine equal, to whom the same
hath happened.

⋆ LXXXII ⋆

ONCHSHESHONQY taught his son:

It is more pleasant to live in your own small house
than to live in the large house of another.
Do not sell your house and your revenues for the sake
of one day, and be poor for ever.
He who enjoys living in his house warms it to the
rafters. He who dislikes it builds one and mortgages
it.

⋆ LXXXIII ⋆

PTAHHOTEP said: Be diligent at all times. Do more than
is commanded. Waste not the time wherein thou
canst labour; he is an abominable man who maketh
a bad use of his time. Lose no chance day by day in
adding to the riches of thy house. Work produceth
wealth, and wealth endureth not when work is
abandoned.

PTAHHOTEP advised: If thou takest to wife one that is well-nurtured, one that is cheerful, one that the people of her city know, put her not away, but give her to eat.

PTAHHOTEP also advised: Act not the official over thy wife in her house, if thou knowest that she is excellent. Say not unto her: 'Where is it? Bring it us,' if she hath put it in the right place. Let thine eye observe and be silent, that thou mayest know her good deeds. She is happy when thine hand is with her. Thereby the man ceaseth to stir up strife in his house.

PTAHHOTEP said: If thou art a wise man, be master of thy house. Love thy wife absolutely, give her food in abundance, and raiment for her back; these are the medicines for her body. She is thy field, and she reflecteth credit on her possessor. Be not harsh in thy house, for she will be more easily moved by persuasion than by violence. Satisfy her wish, observe what she expecteth, and take note of that whereon she hath fixed her gaze. This is the treatment that will keep her in her house; if thou repel her advances, it is ruin for thee.

ONCHSHESHONQY said to his son:

Do not marry an impious woman lest she give your children a bad upbringing.

If a woman is at peace with her husband they shall
never fare badly.
If a woman whispers about her husband they shall
never fare well.
If a woman does not care for the property of her
husband another man is on her mind.
Do not live with your family-in-law.

<h3 style="text-align:center">＊LXXXVIII＊</h3>

PTAHHOTEP warned: If thou wouldst prolong friend-
ship in an house to which thou hast admittance, as
master, or as brother, or as friend, into whatsoever
place thou enterest, beware of approaching the
women. The place where they are is not good.

On that account a thousand go to perdition: Men
are made fools by their gleaming limbs, and lo! they
are already become herset-stones. A trifle, a little, the
likeness of a dream, and death cometh as the end.

<h3 style="text-align:center">＊LXXXIX＊</h3>

THE MAXIMS OF ANI say: Beware of the woman in the
street who is not known in her native town. Follow
her not, nor any woman who is like her. Do not make
her acquaintance. She is like a deep stream the windings
of which are unknown.

<h3 style="text-align:center">＊XC＊</h3>

THE MAXIMS OF ANI say: Follow not after a woman,
and let her not take possession of thy heart.

THE MAXIMS OF ANI say: I gave thee thy mother who bore thee, and in bearing thee she took upon herself a great burden, which she bore without help from me. When after some months thou wast born, she placed herself under a yoke, for three years she suckled thee. When thou wast sent to school to be educated, she brought bread and beer for thee from her house to thy master regularly each day. Thou art now grown up, and thou hast a wife and a house of thy own. Keep thine eye on thy child, and bring him up as thy mother brought thee up. Do nothing whatsoever that will cause her, thy mother, to suffer, least she lift up her hands to God, and he hear her complaint, and punish thee.

THE MAXIMS OF ANI say: Place water before thy father and thy mother who rest in their tombs. . . . Forget not to do this when thou art outside thy house, and as thou doest for them so shall thy son do for thee.

PTAHHOTEP advised: Take to thyself a wife when thou art a youth, that she may give thee a son. Thou shouldest beget him for thee whilst thou art yet young, and shouldest live to see him become a man. Happy is the man who hath much people, and he is respected because of his children.

PTAHHOTEP said: If thou art held in esteem, and hast
an household, and begettest a son that pleaseth God—
if he doeth right, and inclineth to thy nature, and
hearkeneth to thine instruction, and his designs do
good in thine house, and he hath regard for thy substance as it befitteth, search out for him everything
that is good. He is thy son, separate not thine heart
from him. But if he doeth wrong and trespasseth
against thy designs, and acteth not after thine instructions, and his designs are worthless in thine house, and
he defieth all that thou sayest then drive him away,
for he is not thy son.

PTAHHOTEP said: Treat thy dependants as well as thou
art able, for this is the duty of those whom God hath
blessed.

THE MAXIMS OF ANI say: Frequent not the house where
men drink beer, for the words that fall from thy mouth
will be repeated, and it is a bad thing for thee not to
know what thou didst really say. Thou wilt fall down,
thy bones may be broken, and there will be no one to
help thee. When thy friends come to look for thee, they
will find thee lying on the ground as helpless as a babe.

THE MAXIMS OF ANI say: Enter not into the presence
of the drunkard, even if his acquaintance be an honour
to thee.

ONCHSHESHONQY warns: No drunkenness of yesterday removes today's thirst.

THE MAXIMS OF ANI say: Eat not bread, whilst another standeth by, without pointing out to him the bread with thy hand.

KAGEMNI taught: If thou sittest with many persons, hold the food in abhorrence, even if thou desirest it; it taketh only a brief moment to master oneself, and it is disgraceful to be greedy.

As ONCHSHESHONQY pointed out: A snake which is eating has no venom.

The Hymn to the Nile:

Praise to thee, O Nile, that issuest forth from the earth
 and comest to nourish the dwellers in Egypt. Secret
 of movement, a darkness in the daytime.
That waterest the meadows which Re hath created to
 nourish all cattle.
That givest drink to the desert places which are far
 from water; his dew is that falleth from heaven.
Beloved of the Earth-God, controller of the Corn-
 God, that maketh every workshop of Ptah to
 flourish.

Lord of fish, that maketh the water-fowl to go upstream, without a bird falling.

That maketh barley and createth wheat, that maketh
the temples to keep festival.

If he is sluggish the nostrils are stopped up, and all men
are brought low;

The offerings of the gods are diminished, and millions
perish from among mankind;

The greedy man causes confusion throughout the land,
and great and small are brought to naught.

★ CIII ★

MERIKARE was taught: Copy your forefathers, for
work is carried out through knowledge; see, their
words endure in writing. Open, that you may read
and copy knowledge; even the expert will become one
who is instructed.

★ CIV ★

THE STORY of the Shipwrecked Sailor may be the
origin of Sinbad the Sailor:

The wise servant said: Let thy heart be satisfied, O my
lord, for that we have come back to the country; after
we have long been on board, and rowed much, the
prow has at last touched land. All the people rejoice,
and embrace us one after another. Moreover, we have
come back in good health, and not a man is lacking;
although we have been to the ends of Wawat, and
gone through the land of Senmut, we have returned
in peace, and our land—behold, we have come back

to it. Hear me, my lord; I have no other refuge. Wash thee, and turn the water over thy fingers; then go and tell the tale to the majesty.

His lord replied: Thy heart continues still its wandering words! but although the mouth of a man may save him, his words may also cover his face with confusion. Wilt thou do then as thy heart moves thee? This that thou wilt say, tell quietly.

The sailor then answered: Now I shall tell that which has happened to me, to my very self. I was going to the mines of Pharaoh, and I went down on the sea on a ship of 150 cubits long and 40 cubits wide, with 150 sailors of the best of Egypt, who had seen heaven and earth, and whose hearts were stronger than lions. They had said that the wind would not be contrary, or that there would be none. But as we approached the land the wind arose, and threw up waves eight cubits high. As for me I seized a piece of wood; but those who were in the vessel perished, without one remaining. A wave threw me on an island, after that I had been three days alone, without a companion beside my own heart. I laid me in a thicket, and the shadow covered me. Then stretched I my limbs to try to find something for my mouth. I found there figs and grapes, all manner of good herbs, berries and grain, melons of all kinds, fishes and birds. Nothing was lacking. And I satisfied myself; and left on the ground that which was over, of what my arms had been filled withal. I dug a pit, I lighted a fire, and I made a burnt offering unto the gods.

Suddenly I heard a noise as of thunder, which I

thought to be that of a wave of the sea. The trees shook, and the earth was moved. I uncovered my face, and I saw that a serpent drew near. He was thirty cubits long, and his beard greater than two cubits; his body was as overlayed with gold, and his colour as that of true lazuli. He coiled himself before me.

Then he opened his mouth, while that I lay on my face before him, and he said to me, 'What has brought thee, what has brought thee, little one, what has brought thee? If thou sayest not speedily what has brought thee to this isle, I will make thee know thyself; as a flame thou shalt vanish, if thou tellest me not something I have not heard, or which I knew not, before thee.'

Then he took me in his mouth and carried me to his resting-place, and layed me down without any hurt. I was whole and sound, and nothing was gone from me. Then he opened his mouth against me, while that I lay on my face before him, and he said, 'What has brought thee to this isle which is in the sea, and of which the shores are in the midst of the waves?'

Then I replied to him, and holding my arms low before him, I said to him, 'I was embarked for the mines by the order of the majesty. A storm came upon us while we were on the sea. Hardly could we reach to the shore when the wind waxed yet greater, and the waves rose even eight cubits. As for me, I seized a piece of wood, while those who were in the boat perished without one being left with me for three days. Behold me now before thee, for I was brought to this isle by a wave of the sea.'

Then said he to me, 'Fear not, fear not, little one, and make not thy face sad. If thou hast come to me, it is God who has let thee live. For it is he who has brought thee to this isle of the blest, where nothing is lacking, and which is filled with all good things. See now, thou shalt pass one month after another, until thou shalt be four months in this isle. Then a ship shall come from thy land with sailors, and thou shalt leave with them and go to thy country, and thou shalt die in thy town.

'Converse is pleasing, and he who tastes of it passes over his misery. I will therefore tell thee of that which is in this isle. I am here with my brethren and my children around me; we are seventy-five serpents, children, and kindred.

'As for thee if thou art strong, and if thy heart waits patiently, thou shalt press thy infants to thy bosom and embrace thy wife. Thou shalt return to thy house which is full of all good things, thou shalt see thy land, where thou shalt dwell in the midst of thy kindred.'

Then I bowed, in my obeisance, and I touched the ground before him. 'Behold now that which I have told thee before. I shall tell of thy presence unto Pharaoh, I shall make him to know of thy greatness, and I will bring to thee of the sacred oils and perfumes, and of incense of the temples with which all gods are honoured. I shall tell, moreover, of that which I do now see (thanks to him), and there shall be rendered to thee praises before the fullness of all the land. I shall slay asses for thee in sacrifice, I shall pluck for thee the birds, and I shall bring for thee ships full of all kinds

74

of the treasures of Egypt, as is comely to do unto a god, a friend of men in a fair country, of which men know not.'

Then he smiled at my speech, because of that which was in his heart, for he said to me, 'Thou art not rich in perfumes, for all that thou hast is but common incense. As for me I am prince of the land of Punt, and I have perfumes. Only the oil which thou sayedst thou wouldest bring is not common in this isle. But, when thou shalt depart from this place, thou shalt never more see this isle; it shall be changed into waves.'

And, behold, when the ship drew near, according to all that he had told me before, I got me up into an high tree, to strive to see those who were within it. Then I came and told to him this matter; but it was already known unto him before. Then he said to me, 'Farewell, farewell, go to thy house, little one, see again thy children, and let thy name be good in thy town; these are my wishes for thee.'

Then I bowed myself before him, and held my arms low before him, and he, he gave me gifts of precious perfumes, of cassia, of sweet woods, of kohl, of cypress, an abundance of incense, of ivory tusks, of baboons, of apes, and all kind of precious things. I embarked all in the ship which was come, and bowing myself, I prayed God for him.

Then he said to me, 'Behold thou shalt come to thy country in two months, thou shalt press to thy bosom thy children, and thou shalt rest in thy tomb.' After this I went down to the shore unto the ship, and I called to the sailors who were there. Then on the shore

I rendered adoration to the master of this isle and to those who dwelt therein.

When we shall come, in our return, to the house of Pharaoh, in the second month, according to all that the serpent has said, we shall approach unto the palace. And I shall go in before Pharaoh, I shall bring the gifts which I have brought from this isle into the country. Then he shall thank me before the fullness of all the land. Grant then unto me a follower, and lead me to the courtiers of the king. Cast thy eye upon me, after that I am come to land again, after that I have both seen and proved this. Hear my prayer, for it is good to listen to people. It was said unto me, 'Become a wise man, and thou shalt come to honour,' and behold I have become such.

★ CV ★

THE FOLLOWING story is told about the island of Philae: The king's son, Anas el-Wogud, fell in love with the vizier's daughter Zahr el-Ward, 'Flower of the Rose'. The two young people met secretly until they were discovered by the imprudence of the maiden's servant. The vizier was enraged and in order to bring the affair to an end imprisoned his daughter in the temple of Isis under close guard. Anas el-Wogud wandered far and wide in search of his beloved and in the course of his wanderings showed kindness and compassion to animals. One day a hermit told him that Zahr el-Ward was on the island of Philae and Anas hurriedly made his way there. Alas, the water surrounding the island teemed with crocodiles, but as

he stood lamenting his fate one of the monsters offered
to carry him to the island on its back out of gratitude
for the prince's previous kindness to animals. On his
arrival, birds belonging to his sweetheart told him that
she was on the island, but he could never obtain sight
of her. Meanwhile 'Flower of the Rose', unable to
endure her fate, let herself down from her window by
a rope made from her clothes and was conveyed from
the island by a compassionate shipmaster. Finally after
another long period of search the lovers found one
another and with the consent of their families were
happily wed.

★ CVI ★

KING PEPI wrote the following letter: Come north-
ward to the court at once. Thou shalt bring this dwarf
with thee that thou hast brought alive, prosperous and
healthy from the Land of Ghosts, for the dance of the
god, to gladden and rejoice the heart of the King of
Upper and Lower Egypt, Neferkare, Pepi II who
liveth for ever. When he goes down with thee into
the vessel, take care lest he should fall into the water.
When he sleeps at night appoint excellent people to
sleep beside him in the tent, inspect him ten times a
night. My Majesty desires to see this dwarf more than
the gifts of Sinai and of Punt. If thou arrivest at the
court, bringing this dwarf with thee alive and prosperous
and healthy, my Majesty will do for thee a greater thing.

★ CVII ★

DURING a seven-year famine, King Djoser, who built
the Step Pyramid complained: that the Nile had not

risen for seven years and that there was a scarcity of corn. There were no vegetables and no food of any kind, every man was stealing from his neighbour. Counsellors had no advice to give and when the granaries were opened nothing but air issued from them. The king in great distress asked the chief lector-priest of Imhotep: In what place does the Nile rise? What god dwells there, that I may enlist his help? The priest replied that he would consult the sacred writings in the temple of Thoth at Hermopolis. In due course he returned to the Pharaoh and told him that there was a city in the middle of the Nile called Elephantine, which was the seat from which Re despatches life to everyone. It was the source of life, the place from which the Nile leapt forth in its flood to impregnate the lands of Egypt. On the east side of the city were great mountains containing hard stone which was used in the temples of Upper and Lower Egypt. The priest continued that the god of the place was Khnum, who allotted the lands of Egypt to each god and con-trolled the grain, the birds, the fish and everything on which they live. Some days later, King Djoser had a dream in which the great god Khnum appeared. The king did everything he could to render the god favourable, but Khnum replied: 'I am Khnum your maker; with my arms I protect you and help you. You should be building temples and restoring my statues and those buildings that have fallen into ruin; I am Nun who has existed from earliest times; I am the Nile flood who runs at will; my sanctuary has two gates from which I let out the water for the flood.'

Khnum continued that he would make the flood rise for the king, that want would cease and the granaries be filled. When the king awoke he remembered the dream and set about restoring the damage that had been done. He decreed that large tracts of land on both sides of the river stretching from Elephantine south should be given to the temple of Khnum. In addition one-tenth of all produce and livestock raised was to be given to the temple, and also taxes on caravans and gold mining. 'Such are the terms of my decree,' said King Djoser, 'and I order that it be inscribed on a stone set up in a sacred place, and I also order that the priests shall make my name live eternally in the temple of Khnum, Lord of Elephantine.'

⋆ CVIII ⋆

A PROCLAMATION by Tutankhamun restored the old religion after the reign of Akhenaten: When His Majesty arose as king, the temples of the gods and goddesses, beginning from Elephantine down to the marshes of the Delta had fallen into decay, their shrines had fallen into desolation and become ruins overgrown with weeds, their chapels as though they had never been and their halls serving as footpaths. The land was topsy-turvy and the gods turned their backs on this land. If messengers were sent to Djahi [Syria] to extend the boundaries of Egypt, they had no success. If one humbled oneself to a god to ask a thing from him, he did not come, and if prayer was made to a goddess, likewise she never came. But after many days My Majesty arose from the seat of his father and ruled over the territories of Horus, the Black Land and the Red Land being under his supervision.

RAMESSES IV, grandson of the builder of Abu Simbel, prayed to Osiris: And thou shalt give me health, life and old age, a long reign and strength to all my limbs; sight to my eyes, hearing to my ears and pleasure to my heart daily. And thou shalt give me to eat to satiety, and thou shalt give me to drink to drunkenness, and thou shalt promote my seed to be kings in this country to eternity and for ever. And thou shalt make me content every day, thou shalt listen to my voice in whatsoever I shall say to thee and grant me very high Nile floods to furnish thy offerings and to furnish the offerings of the gods and goddesses, the lords of Northern and Southern Egypt, to preserve the sacred bulls, to preserve all the people of thy lands, their cattle and their trees which thy hand has made. For it is thou who hast made them all; thou canst not abandon them to pursue another design with them, for that would not be right.

THE STORY is told of Ramesses the Great in the Battle of Kadesh: Then His Majesty arose like his father Mont and took the accoutrements of battle, and girt himself with his corselet; he was like Baal in his hour, and the great pair of horses which bore His Majesty, belonging to the great stable of Usimaresetpentre, beloved of Amun, were named Victory-in-Thebes. Then His Majesty started forth at a gallop, and entered into the host of the fallen ones of Khatti, being alone by himself, none other with him. And His Majesty went to look about him, and found surrounding him on his outer side 2,500 pairs of horses with all the champions of the fallen ones of Khatti and of the many countries who were with them, from Arzawa, Masa, Pidasa, Keshkesh, Arwen, Kizzuwadna, Khaleb, Ugarit, Kadesh, and Luka; they were three men to a pair of horses as a unit, whereas there was no captain with me, no charioteer, no soldier of the army, no shield-bearer; my infantry and chariotry melted away before them, not one of them stood firm to fight with them. Then said His Majesty: What ails thee, my father Amun? Is it a father's part to ignore his son? Have I done anything without thee, do I not walk and halt at thy bidding? I have not disobeyed any course commanded by thee. How great is the great lord of Egypt to allow foreigners to draw nigh in his path! What careth thy heart, O Amun, for these Asiatics so ignorant of God? Have I not made for thee very many monuments and filled thy temple with my booty, and built for thee my Mansion of Millions of Years and given thee all my wealth as a permanent possession and presented to thee all lands together to enrich thy offerings, and have caused to be sacrificed to thee tens of thousands of cattle and all manner of sweet-scented herbs? No good deeds have I left un-done. What will men say if even a little thing befall him who bends himself to thy counsel?

Fortified by his prayers to Amun, Ramesses rallied his shield-bearer, Menna, who not unnaturally was intimidated by the odds of 2,500 to 1. The poem continues with Menna saying:

'My good Lord, thou strong Ruler, thou great saviour of Egypt on the day of fighting, we stand alone in the midst of the battle. Behold, the infantry and chariotry have deserted us, for what reason dost though remain to rescue them? Let us get clear and do thou save us, O Usimaresetpentre.' Then said His Majesty to his shield-bearer: 'Stand firm, steady thy heart, my shield-bearer. I will enter in among them like the pounce of a falcon, killing, slaughtering, and casting to the ground. What careth thy heart for these effeminate ones at millions of whom I take no pleasure?' Thereupon His Majesty started forth quickly and entered at a gallop into the midst of the battle for the sixth time of entering in amongst them.

(Sir Alan Gardiner, *Egypt of the Pharaohs*)

★ CXI ★

THE STORY of the battle of Kadesh is told on the monuments of Karnak, Luxor, Abydos and the Ramesseum, which also contains the largest and heaviest statue of Ramesses. It is of this statue, now sadly fallen and defaced, that Shelley wrote his poem *Ozymandias*:

I met a traveller from an antique land
  Who said: Two vast and trunkless legs of stone
Stand in the desert . . . Near them on the sand,

Half sunk, a shattered visage lies, whose frown,
And wrinkled lip and sneer of cold command,
Tell that its sculptor well those passions read
Which yet survive, stamped on these lifeless things,
The hand that mocked them, and the heart that fed.
And on the pedestal these words appear:
'My name is Ozymandias, king of kings:
Look on my works, ye Mighty, and despair!'
Nothing beside remains. Round the decay
Of that colossal wreck, boundless and bare,
The lone and level sands stretch far away.

★ CXII ★

THE MAN WHO WAS TIRED OF LIFE wrote:

To whom can I speak today?
Faces are averted,
And every man looks askance at his brethren.

To whom can I speak today?
Hearts are rapacious
And there is no man's heart in which one can trust.

To whom can I speak today?
There are no just persons
And the land is left over to the doers of wrong.

★ CXIII ★

THE STORY of The Blinding of Truth by Falsehood is
told as follows: A knife which Falsehood had entrusted
to his brother, Truth, had somehow been lost or
damaged. When Truth offered to replace it, Falsehood
claimed it was impossible because of its size and value.

Acting on Falsehood's demand the tribunal of the gods condemned Truth to be blinded and to become Falsehood's door-keeper. After some further adventures Truth begat a son who, when he grew up, determined to avenge his father. Having picked a quarrel with Falsehood over the possession of an ox, the boy took him to the divine tribunal and by a trick obtained the verdict. As a punishment Falsehood was beaten and blinded and made to serve as Truth's door-keeper.

* CXIV *

THE SONG OF THE HARPER is found on the wall of an Egyptian tomb:

Rejoice and let thy heart forget that day when they shall lay thee to rest.

Cast all sorrow behind thee, and bethink thee of joy until there come that day of reaching port in the land that loveth silence.

Follow thy desire as long as thou livest, put myrrh on thy head, clothe thee in fine linen.

Set singing and music before thy face.

Increase yet more the delights which thou hast, and let not thy heart grow faint. Follow thine inclination and thy profit. Do thy desires upon earth, and trouble not thine heart until that day of lamentation come to thee.

Spend a happy day and weary not thereof. Lo, none may take his goods with him, and none that hath gone may come again.

FURTHER READING

Budge, E. W., *The Literature of the Egyptians*. Dent 1914.

Cerny, J., *Ancient Egyptian Religion*. Hutchinson 1952.

Edwards, A. B., *A Thousand Miles up the Nile*. London 1877.

Erman, A., *Literature of the Ancient Egyptians*. 1927; Arno 1968.

Flinders Petrie, W. M., *Egyptian Tales*. Methuen 1899.

Gardiner, A. H., *Egypt of the Pharaohs*. Oxford 1961.

James, T. G. H., *Myths and Legends of Ancient Egypt*. Hamlyn 1969.

James, T. G. H., *Archaeology of Ancient Egypt*. Bodley Head 1972.

Kees, H., *Ancient Egypt, A Cultural Topography*. London 1961.

MacQuitty, William, *Tutankhamun, The Last Journey*. Crown 1977.

MacQuitty, William, *Island of Isis*. Scribner's 1976.

MacQuitty, William, *Ramesses the Great, Master of the World*. Mitchell Beazley 1978.

Simpson, W. K. ed., *The Literature of Ancient Egypt*. Yale University Press 1972.

Introductory Guide to the Egyptian Collections. British Museum 1964.